A CATS STEAMPUNK ALPHABET

A CATS STEAMPUNK ALPHABET

words by G.D. Falksen
illustrations by Evelyn Kriete
foreword by Jay Lake

WILDSIDE PRESS

"English cats that do not look and live like Louis Wain cats
are ashamed of themselves." —H.G. Wells.

Special thanks to British artist LOUIS WAIN (1860-1939),
whose beautiful cat illustrations form the heart of the
collages in this collection.

Foreword

by Jay Lake

About four years ago, I mentioned on my blog that a steampunk abecedary would be a very cool thing. It started out literally as a joke, a bloggy game of the kind I like to play with my readers from time to time. Except in the real world jokes have a way of taking on a life of

their own, mutating and metastasizing into things the originally wiseacre might never recognize.

Steampunk has a way of doing that. The aesthetic has strong roots in the literature of the fantastic, but it's been taken over and remade by the Maker movement, as well as costuming, music, visual arts, culture, games and movies. Purposing and repurposing and depurposing and recontextualizing are all

of a piece as steampunk appropriates from the main strands of Victorian and Edwardian culture, then fills in the gaps and cross threads with influences from around the world and even other suns.

Here you have a concrete example of that tendency. Evelyn Kriete and G.D. Falksen are a pair of die-hard steampunks who decided not to let my idea die hard. Evelyn and Geoff ran with the steampunk abecedary, taking my throwaway

bit of Thursday morning humor and eventually transforming it into the book you now hold in your hands. You'll see how their art and artistry combine with the sly wit and humor that infuse much of the steampunk movement.

I claim no credit for this book. (Which, put more plainly, means a plaintive wail of "It's not my fault, I swear!") All I claim is that a shared idea blossomed into something distinctive, entertaining and beautiful.

Enjoy. And count the letters carefully. This is steampunk, after all. You don't know what might have snuck in.

— Jay Lake
Portland, OR

A for Airship,
for flying is keen

B is for Boiler,
turning water to steam

C is for Coal,
feeding the fire

D for Dirigible,
floating higher and higher

E is for Engine,
an invention quite droll

F is for Fireman,
shoveling coal

G is for Gear,
which guides the machine

H for Hydraulic,
a power unseen

I is for Iron,
companion to steel

J is for Jingo,
an expression of zeal

K, Kilimanjaro, an adventure of worth

L, then, for Landship,
dreadnought of the earth

M is for Motor,
a gentleman's toy

N is for Nation,
empire's ploy

O is for Oil,
the future of fuel

P is for Pith helm,
to keep the head cool

Q is for Quarry,
let the hunter engage

R is for Railroad,
the jewel of the age

S is for Steam,
driving it all

T is for Timepiece,
in pocket, on wall

U for Umbrella,
let none be without

V for the Vicar,
let's hope he's devout

W for Winch,
to magnify might

X for Xenophobia,
I hear the French bite

Y is for Yellow,
journalism of vice

Z is for Zenith,
   isn't empire nice?